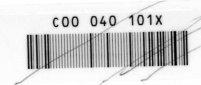
2

LOOK INSIDE
CROSS-SECTIONS
TANKS

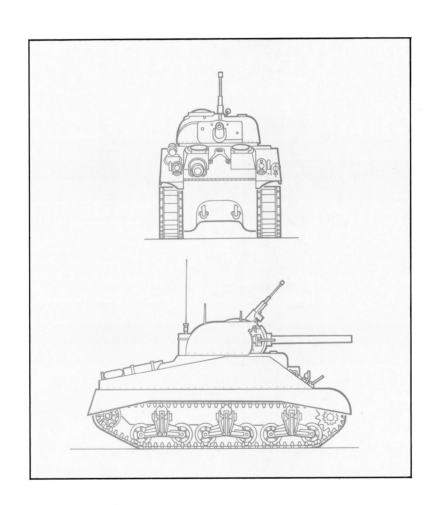

LOOK INSIDE
CROSS-SECTIONS
TANKS

ILLUSTRATED BY
RICHARD CHASEMORE

WRITTEN BY
IAN HARVEY

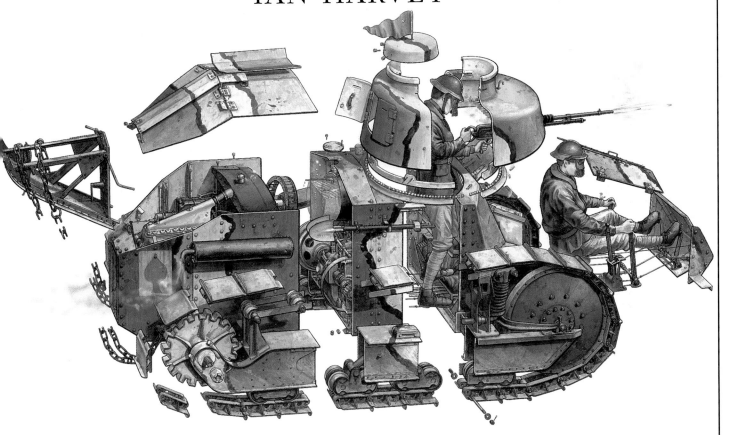

DORLING KINDERSLEY
LONDON • NEW YORK • STUTTGART

A DORLING KINDERSLEY BOOK

Senior Art Editor Dorian Spencer Davies
Designer Joanne Earl
Senior Editor John C. Miles
Editorial Assistant Nigel Ritchie
Deputy Art Director Miranda Kennedy
Deputy Editorial Director Sophie Mitchell
Production Charlotte Traill
Consultant David Fletcher
The Tank Museum
Bovington, Dorset

First published in 1996
by Dorling Kindersley Limited,
9 Henrietta Street, London WC2E 8PS

A CIP catalogue record for this book is available
from the British Library

ISBN 0-7513-5438-4

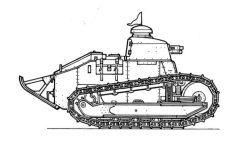

Reproduced by Dot Gradations, Essex
Printed and bound in Belgium by Proost

CONTENTS

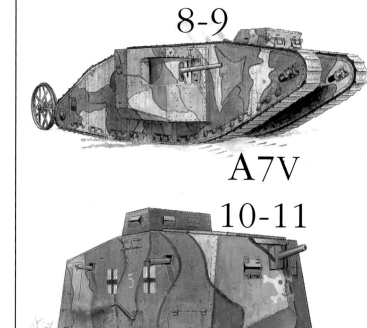

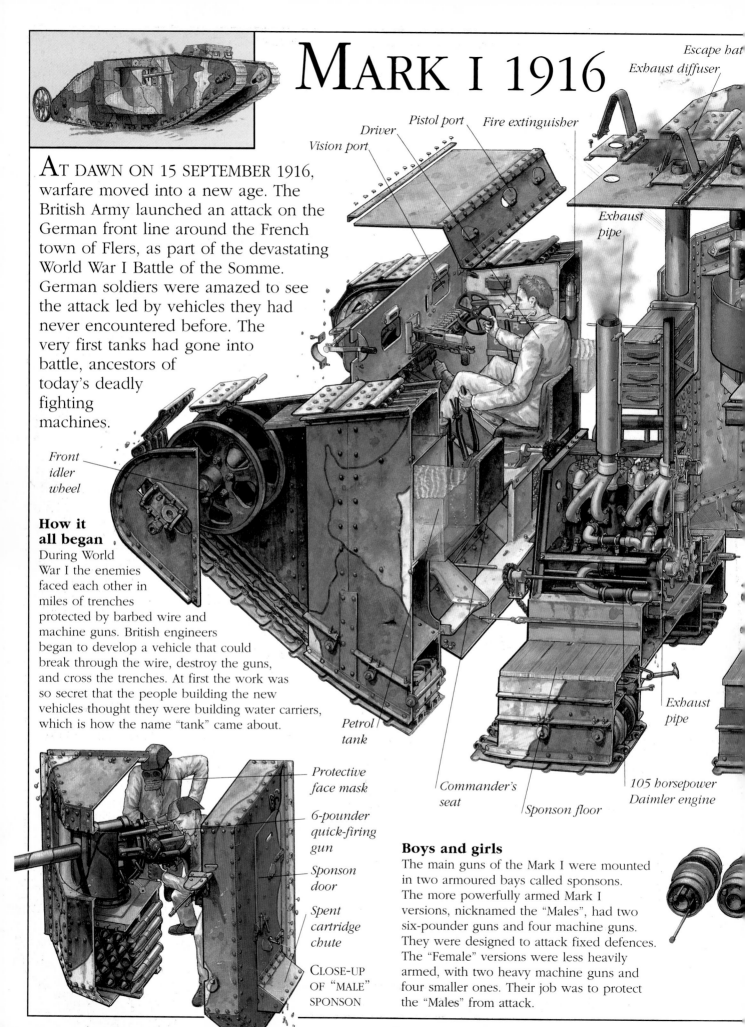

MARK I 1916

At dawn on 15 September 1916, warfare moved into a new age. The British Army launched an attack on the German front line around the French town of Flers, as part of the devastating World War I Battle of the Somme. German soldiers were amazed to see the attack led by vehicles they had never encountered before. The very first tanks had gone into battle, ancestors of today's deadly fighting machines.

How it all began

During World War I the enemies faced each other in miles of trenches protected by barbed wire and machine guns. British engineers began to develop a vehicle that could break through the wire, destroy the guns, and cross the trenches. At first the work was so secret that the people building the new vehicles thought they were building water carriers, which is how the name "tank" came about.

Escape hat

Exhaust diffuser

Driver

Pistol port

Fire extinguisher

Vision port

Exhaust pipe

Front idler wheel

Exhaust pipe

Petrol tank

Commander's seat

Sponson floor

105 horsepower Daimler engine

Protective face mask

6-pounder quick-firing gun

Sponson door

Spent cartridge chute

CLOSE-UP OF "MALE" SPONSON

Boys and girls

The main guns of the Mark I were mounted in two armoured bays called sponsons. The more powerfully armed Mark I versions, nicknamed the "Males", had two six-pounder guns and four machine guns. They were designed to attack fixed defences. The "Female" versions were less heavily armed, with two heavy machine guns and four smaller ones. Their job was to protect the "Males" from attack.

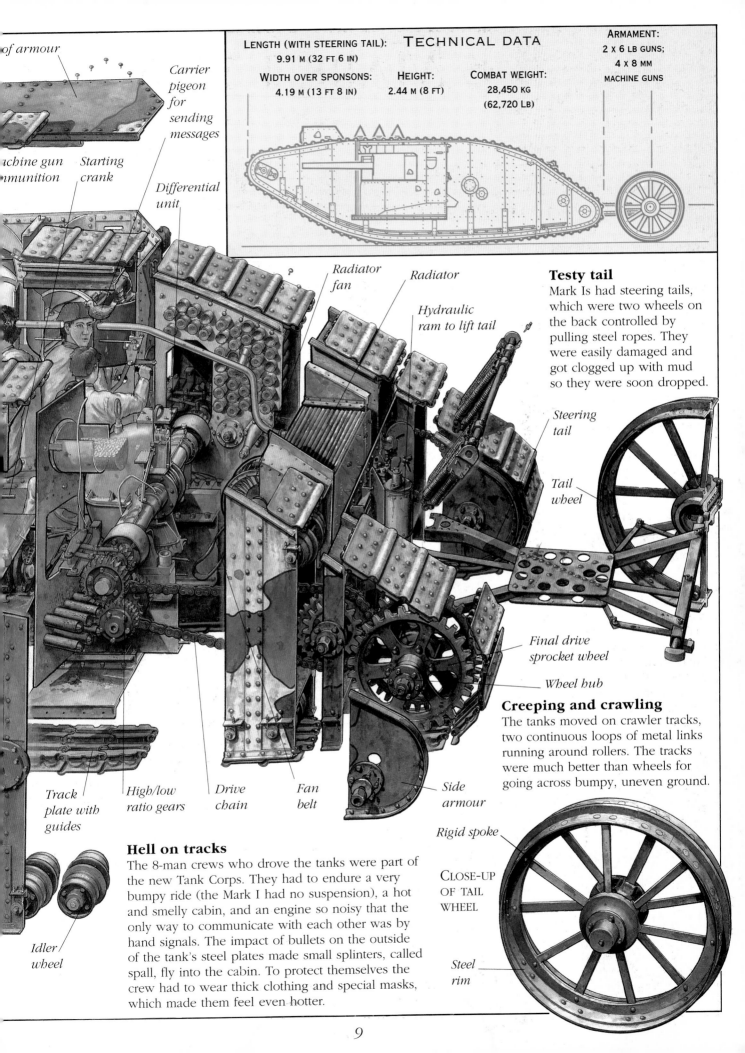

of armour

Carrier pigeon for sending messages

machine gun ammunition

Starting crank

Differential unit

TECHNICAL DATA

LENGTH (WITH STEERING TAIL):
9.91 M (32 FT 6 IN)

WIDTH OVER SPONSONS:
4.19 M (13 FT 8 IN)

HEIGHT:
2.44 M (8 FT)

COMBAT WEIGHT:
28,450 KG
(62,720 LB)

ARMAMENT:
2 X 6 LB GUNS;
4 X 8 MM
MACHINE GUNS

Radiator fan

Radiator

Hydraulic ram to lift tail

Testy tail

Mark Is had steering tails, which were two wheels on the back controlled by pulling steel ropes. They were easily damaged and got clogged up with mud so they were soon dropped.

Steering tail

Tail wheel

Final drive sprocket wheel

Wheel hub

Creeping and crawling

The tanks moved on crawler tracks, two continuous loops of metal links running around rollers. The tracks were much better than wheels for going across bumpy, uneven ground.

Track plate with guides

High/low ratio gears

Drive chain

Fan belt

Side armour

Idler wheel

Rigid spoke

CLOSE-UP OF TAIL WHEEL

Steel rim

Hell on tracks

The 8-man crews who drove the tanks were part of the new Tank Corps. They had to endure a very bumpy ride (the Mark I had no suspension), a hot and smelly cabin, and an engine so noisy that the only way to communicate with each other was by hand signals. The impact of bullets on the outside of the tank's steel plates made small splinters, called spall, fly into the cabin. To protect themselves the crew had to wear thick clothing and special masks, which made them feel even hotter.

9

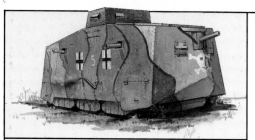

A7V

WHEN THE GERMAN FORCES SAW THE new Allied tanks they quickly set about making a version of their own. They chose to build giant-sized and in 1917 they began to make the A7V *Sturmpanzerwagen*, which was more like a large armoured fortress. It carried 18 men and was heavily armed, but it moved slowly and was no good for climbing steep slopes or crossing trenches. On 24 April 1918, military history was made when the first tank battle took place between A7Vs and British Mark IVs (developed versions of the Mark I).

Guns aplenty

In the crowded A7V there was a commander, a driver and two mechanics, two men manning the main gun, and twelve machine-gunners. It travelled at a top speed of about 9 km/h (5 mph) but it made up for its slowness with lots of firepower. Its main gun was a 57 mm cannon and it had six 7.92 mm machine guns positioned round the sides and at the back. That meant it could fire shells and spray a deadly hail of bullets.

Cross-country clodhopper

The A7V did not travel well over uneven ground. Its tracks were short and they didn't rise up at the front like the Allied tanks, which meant it could only clear a small slope or a narrow trench. The bottom of the tank was very close to the ground so it could easily get stuck on bumps. To add to its problems it was very heavy, so its engines overheated and wore out quickly.

Cupola

Commander

Driver

Steering wheel

Driver's pedal

Roof armour plate

Gun loader

57 mm gun

57 mm gun barrel

Elevating handwheel

Gunner

57 mm gun ammunition box

Gun pedestal

Fuel tank

Front idler wheel

Track bogie

Engine radiator

Exhaust silencer

Exhaust pipe

Daimler engine

TECHNICAL DATA

LENGTH:	HEIGHT:	ARMAMENT:	WIDTH:
8 M (26 FT 3 IN)	3.5 M (11 FT 6 IN)	1 x 57 MM GUN; 6 x 7.92 MM MACHINE GUNS	3.2 M (10 FT 6 IN)

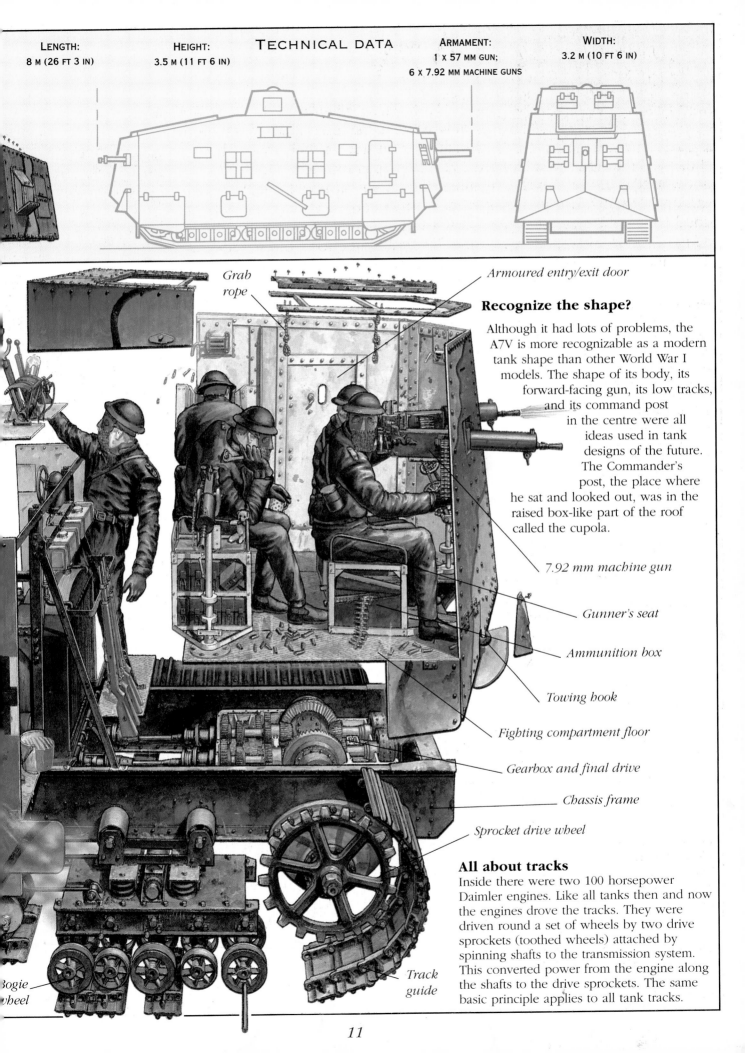

Grab rope

Armoured entry/exit door

Recognize the shape?

Although it had lots of problems, the A7V is more recognizable as a modern tank shape than other World War I models. The shape of its body, its forward-facing gun, its low tracks, and its command post in the centre were all ideas used in tank designs of the future. The Commander's post, the place where he sat and looked out, was in the raised box-like part of the roof called the cupola.

7.92 mm machine gun

Gunner's seat

Ammunition box

Towing hook

Fighting compartment floor

Gearbox and final drive

Chassis frame

Sprocket drive wheel

All about tracks

Inside there were two 100 horsepower Daimler engines. Like all tanks then and now the engines drove the tracks. They were driven round a set of wheels by two drive sprockets (toothed wheels) attached by spinning shafts to the transmission system. This converted power from the engine along the shafts to the drive sprockets. The same basic principle applies to all tank tracks.

Track guide

Bogie wheel

WHIPPET

THE MARK I TANKS COULD BREAK through a front line of trenches but they were too slow to go much further. A lighter, faster tank was needed, one that could penetrate further behind the line and do more damage. Officially this new design, the first ever light tank, was called the Medium Tank Mark A. It soon became known to everyone as the "Whippet", nicknamed after the small but lightning-fast whippet breed of dog. Whippets were first used near the end of the war in 1918 and they lived up to their nickname during the Battle of Amiens when they managed to get nearly 16 km (10 miles) behind enemy lines.

Double trouble
At 14,225 kg (14 tons) the Whippet was half the weight of a Mark I and it could cruise along at twice the speed – up to 13 km/h (8 mph). At the front of the tank there were two 45 horsepower engines, each one driving a crawler track.

Turning
The Whippet was steered by running one track more quickly than the other, using two clutches and two gearboxes. This needed a skilful driver – it was rather like driving two cars at once!

Turret time
The Whippet was the first tank ever to have a raised turret, called a barbette. Although it could not turn around, the tank's crew were able to fire their machine guns through the many gunports.

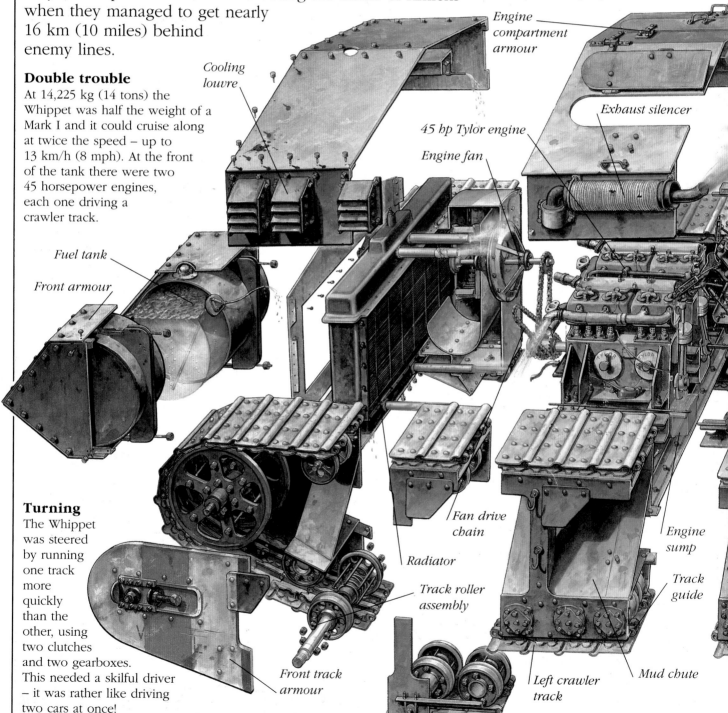

Cooling louvre

Engine compartment armour

45 hp Tylor engine

Exhaust silencer

Engine fan

Fuel tank

Front armour

Fan drive chain

Radiator

Track roller assembly

Engine sump

Track guide

Front track armour

Left crawler track

Mud chute

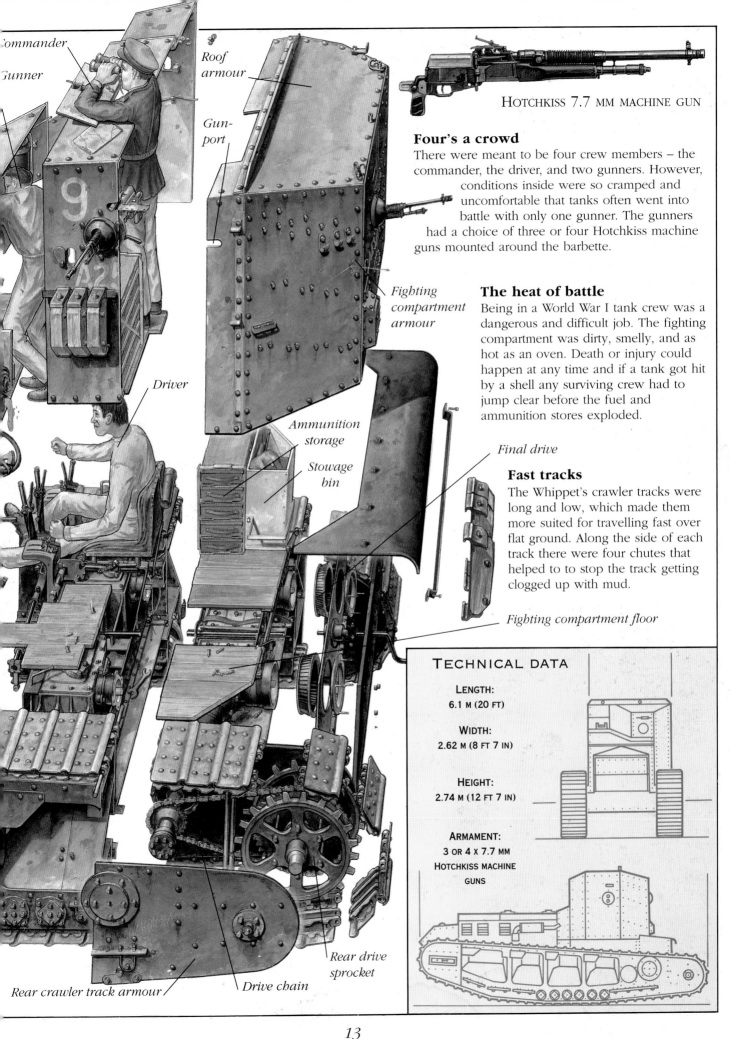

Commander

Gunner

Roof armour

Gun-port

9

HOTCHKISS 7.7 MM MACHINE GUN

Four's a crowd

There were meant to be four crew members – the commander, the driver, and two gunners. However, conditions inside were so cramped and uncomfortable that tanks often went into battle with only one gunner. The gunners had a choice of three or four Hotchkiss machine guns mounted around the barbette.

Fighting compartment armour

The heat of battle

Being in a World War I tank crew was a dangerous and difficult job. The fighting compartment was dirty, smelly, and as hot as an oven. Death or injury could happen at any time and if a tank got hit by a shell any surviving crew had to jump clear before the fuel and ammunition stores exploded.

Driver

Ammunition storage

Stowage bin

Final drive

Fast tracks

The Whippet's crawler tracks were long and low, which made them more suited for travelling fast over flat ground. Along the side of each track there were four chutes that helped to to stop the track getting clogged up with mud.

Fighting compartment floor

Rear crawler track armour

Drive chain

Rear drive sprocket

TECHNICAL DATA

LENGTH:
6.1 M (20 FT)

WIDTH:
2.62 M (8 FT 7 IN)

HEIGHT:
2.74 M (12 FT 7 IN)

ARMAMENT:
3 OR 4 X 7.7 MM
HOTCHKISS MACHINE
GUNS

RENAULT FT17

DURING WORLD WAR I, THE FRENCH ALSO HAD CLEVER engineers developing tanks for them. One of their best designs was the Renault FT17, introduced in 1918. It was a light fast tank which was designed to be used as part of a group leading infantry through a hole in trench defences made by bigger tanks. It was also good for racing ahead to spy out the land for the infantry. Because it was light, it wasn't very successful on bumpy trench-filled ground, but it was ideal for fighting out in open spaces. It was so popular that lots of other countries soon began to buy it after the war.

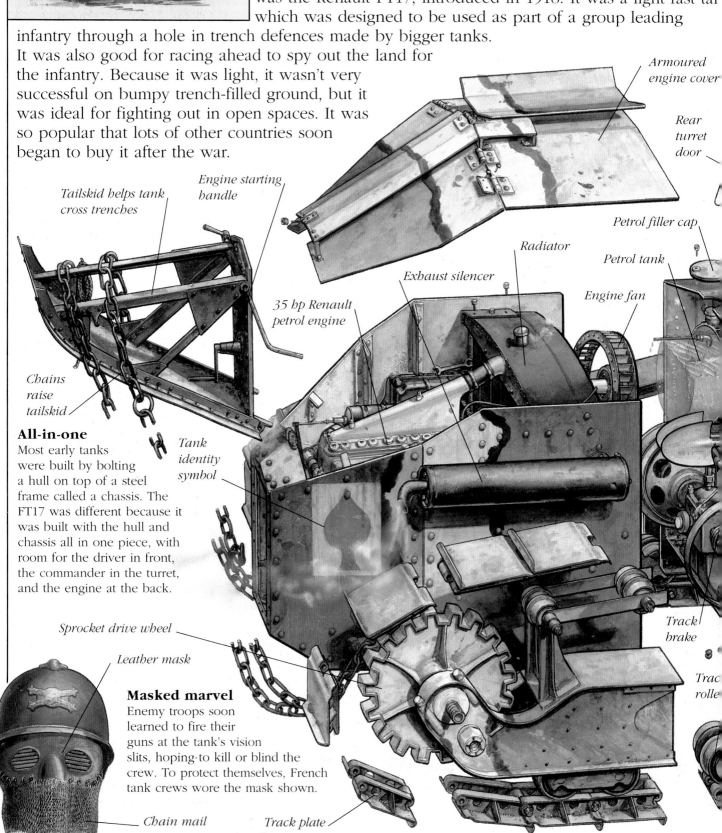

Armoured engine cover

Rear turret door

Tailskid helps tank cross trenches

Engine starting handle

Petrol filler cap

Radiator

Petrol tank

Exhaust silencer

Engine fan

35 hp Renault petrol engine

Chains raise tailskid

All-in-one
Most early tanks were built by bolting a hull on top of a steel frame called a chassis. The FT17 was different because it was built with the hull and chassis all in one piece, with room for the driver in front, the commander in the turret, and the engine at the back.

Tank identity symbol

Track brake

Sprocket drive wheel

Leather mask

Track roller

Masked marvel
Enemy troops soon learned to fire their guns at the tank's vision slits, hoping to kill or blind the crew. To protect themselves, French tank crews wore the mask shown.

Chain mail

Track plate

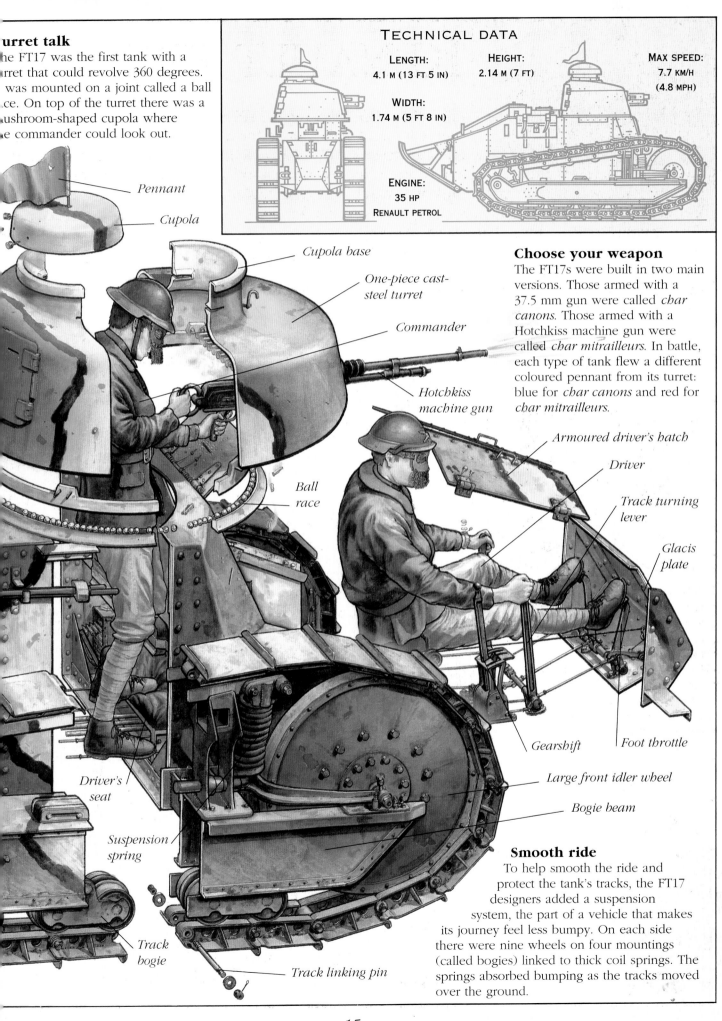

urret talk

he FT17 was the first tank with a
rret that could revolve 360 degrees.
was mounted on a joint called a ball
ce. On top of the turret there was a
ushroom-shaped cupola where
e commander could look out.

TECHNICAL DATA

LENGTH:
4.1 M (13 FT 5 IN)

HEIGHT:
2.14 M (7 FT)

MAX SPEED:
7.7 KM/H
(4.8 MPH)

WIDTH:
1.74 M (5 FT 8 IN)

ENGINE:
35 HP
RENAULT PETROL

Pennant

Cupola

Cupola base

One-piece cast-
steel turret

Commander

Hotchkiss
machine gun

Ball
race

Driver's
seat

Suspension
spring

Track
bogie

Track linking pin

Choose your weapon

The FT17s were built in two main
versions. Those armed with a
37.5 mm gun were called *char
canons*. Those armed with a
Hotchkiss machine gun were
called *char mitrailleurs*. In battle,
each type of tank flew a different
coloured pennant from its turret:
blue for *char canons* and red for
char mitrailleurs.

Armoured driver's hatch

Driver

Track turning
lever

Glacis
plate

Gearshift

Foot throttle

Large front idler wheel

Bogie beam

Smooth ride

To help smooth the ride and
protect the tank's tracks, the FT17
designers added a suspension
system, the part of a vehicle that makes
its journey feel less bumpy. On each side
there were nine wheels on four mountings
(called bogies) linked to thick coil springs. The
springs absorbed bumping as the tracks moved
over the ground.

RUSSIAN T-34

IN 1939 THE WORLD WENT TO WAR AGAIN AND THIS time the Germans used tanks very effectively in their *Blitzkrieg*, or "lightning war." Their Panzer tanks rolled across Europe and pushed deep into Russia, but as they fell back, the Russians were already preparing a surprise to help stop their enemies – the T-34 tank. It was fast and thickly armoured, with a gun so powerful and accurate that it could knock out enemy tanks before they got near enough to return fire.

Dual role

The T-34 had a crew of four, with the commander also acting as gunner. This meant that he was overworked and did neither job as well as he might. The inside of the tank was simple and easy to operate. That was just as well because sometimes new T-34 crews had only three days of training before they were sent into battle.

Armour

The surfaces of the T-34 hull were sloped so that shot would be more likely to bounce off it rather than penetrate inside. In later models its turret was cast in one piece instead of being made up from several sections, and that meant it could withstand attack more easily than the German PzKpfw III tanks it met in battle. By the end of its production, T-34 frontal turret armour was 65 mm (2.5 in) thick.

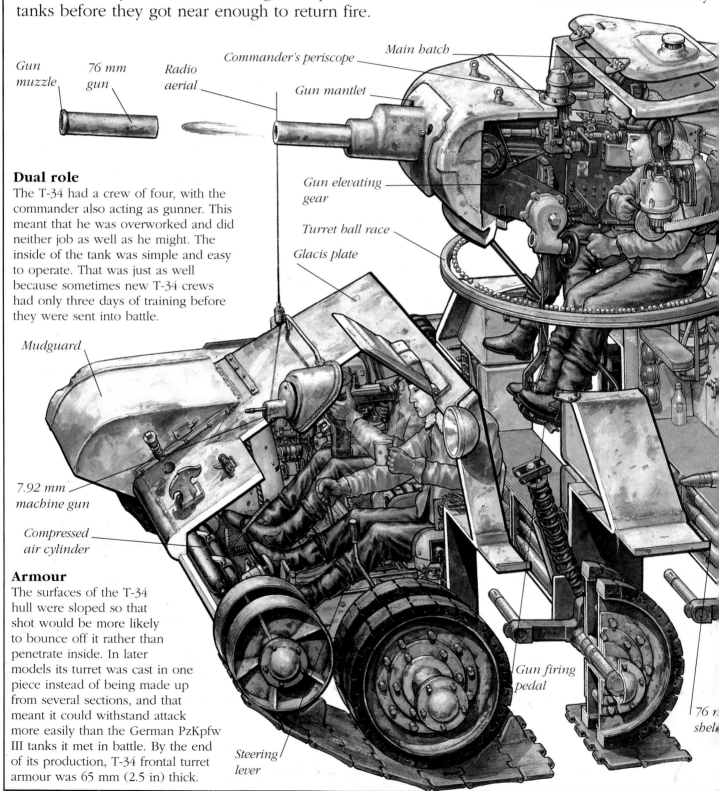

Gun muzzle

76 mm gun

Radio aerial

Commander's periscope

Main hatch

Gun mantlet

Gun elevating gear

Turret ball race

Glacis plate

Mudguard

7.92 mm machine gun

Compressed air cylinder

Gun firing pedal

76 mm shell

Steering lever

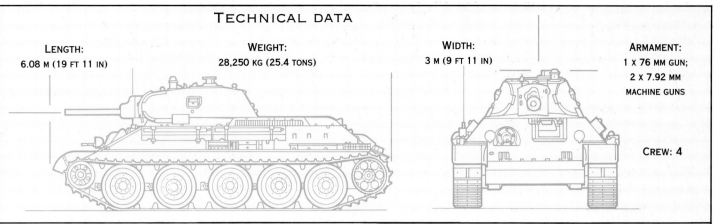

TECHNICAL DATA

LENGTH:	WEIGHT:	WIDTH:	ARMAMENT:
6.08 M (19 FT 11 IN)	28,250 KG (25.4 TONS)	3 M (9 FT 11 IN)	1 x 76 MM GUN; 2 x 7.92 MM MACHINE GUNS
			CREW: 4

Anti freeze features

The engine ran on diesel fuel, which meant it wouldn't freeze up in the depths of a Russian winter. It had an electric starter motor, and if this didn't work in cold weather the crew could start the engine using compressed air stored in cylinders at the front of the tank.

Moving the lot

The first T-34s were built in factories in Leningrad, Kharkov, and Stalingrad. As the Germans advanced towards these places, the Russians dismantled the Leningrad and Kharkov factories piece by piece and moved them to faraway Siberia, where they were rebuilt. They were combined on a site that became known as "Tankograd". At Stalingrad, the tanks continued to be made and were driven straight off the assembly line into the battle raging nearby.

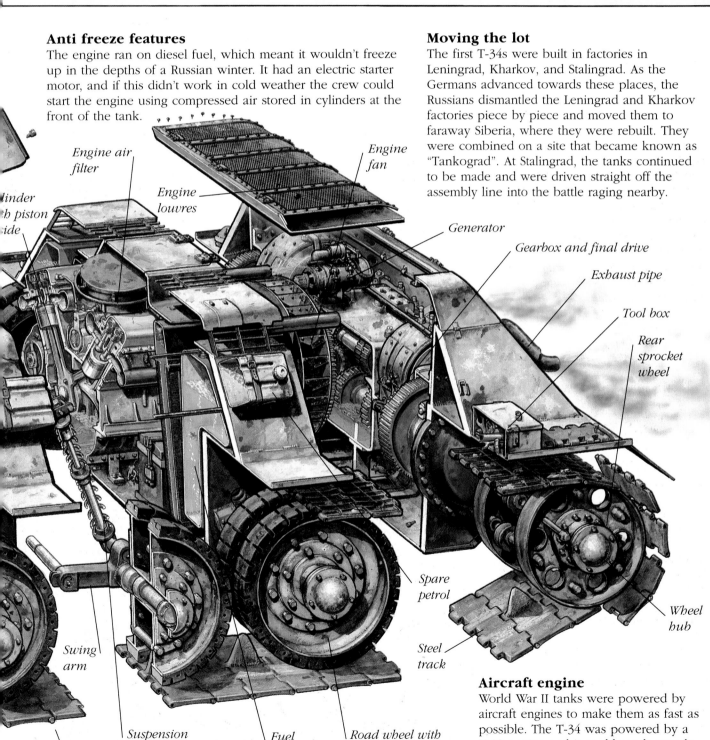

Engine air filter

Engine louvres

Engine fan

linder h piston ide

Generator

Gearbox and final drive

Exhaust pipe

Tool box

Rear sprocket wheel

Spare petrol

Steel track

Wheel hub

Swing arm

Track pin

Suspension spring

Fuel tank

Road wheel with solid rubber tyre

Aircraft engine

World War II tanks were powered by aircraft engines to make them as fast as possible. The T-34 was powered by a V-12 engine and it could reach speeds up to 50 km/h (30 mph) on a good road.

CHURCHILL

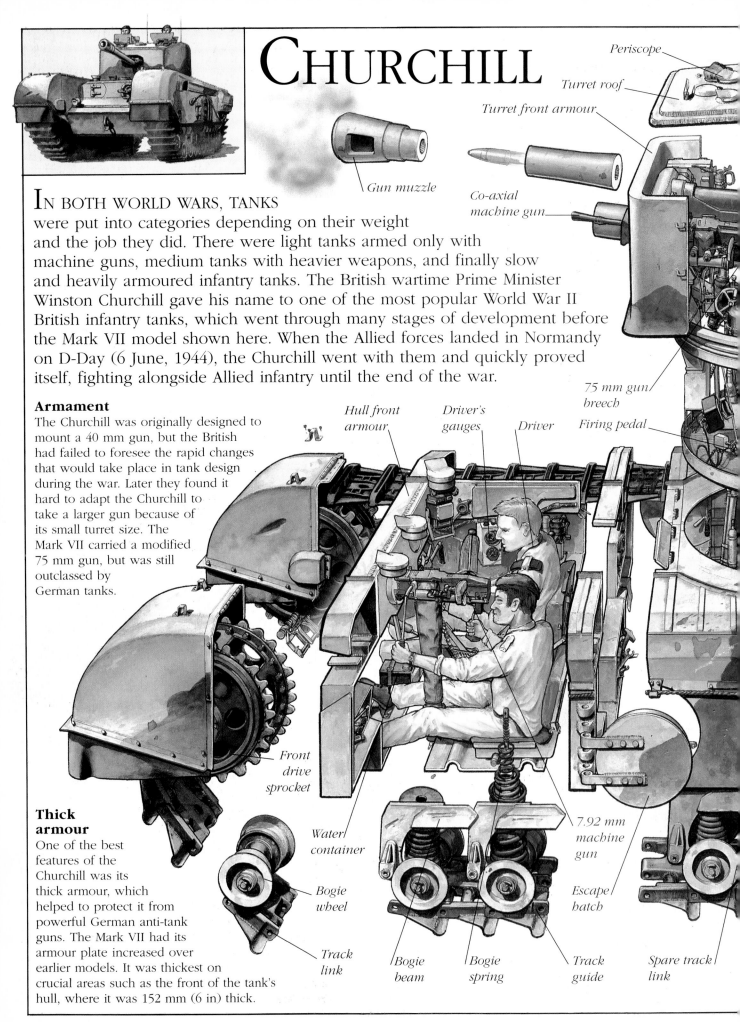

Periscope

Turret roof

Turret front armour

Gun muzzle

Co-axial
machine gun

IN BOTH WORLD WARS, TANKS
were put into categories depending on their weight
and the job they did. There were light tanks armed only with
machine guns, medium tanks with heavier weapons, and finally slow
and heavily armoured infantry tanks. The British wartime Prime Minister
Winston Churchill gave his name to one of the most popular World War II
British infantry tanks, which went through many stages of development before
the Mark VII model shown here. When the Allied forces landed in Normandy
on D-Day (6 June, 1944), the Churchill went with them and quickly proved
itself, fighting alongside Allied infantry until the end of the war.

75 mm gun
breech

Armament

The Churchill was originally designed to
mount a 40 mm gun, but the British
had failed to foresee the rapid changes
that would take place in tank design
during the war. Later they found it
hard to adapt the Churchill to
take a larger gun because of
its small turret size. The
Mark VII carried a modified
75 mm gun, but was still
outclassed by
German tanks.

Hull front
armour

Driver's
gauges

Driver

Firing pedal

Front
drive
sprocket

Thick
armour

One of the best
features of the
Churchill was its
thick armour, which
helped to protect it from
powerful German anti-tank
guns. The Mark VII had its
armour plate increased over
earlier models. It was thickest on
crucial areas such as the front of the tank's
hull, where it was 152 mm (6 in) thick.

Water
container

Bogie
wheel

Track
link

Bogie
beam

Bogie
spring

7.92 mm
machine
gun

Escape
hatch

Track
guide

Spare track
link

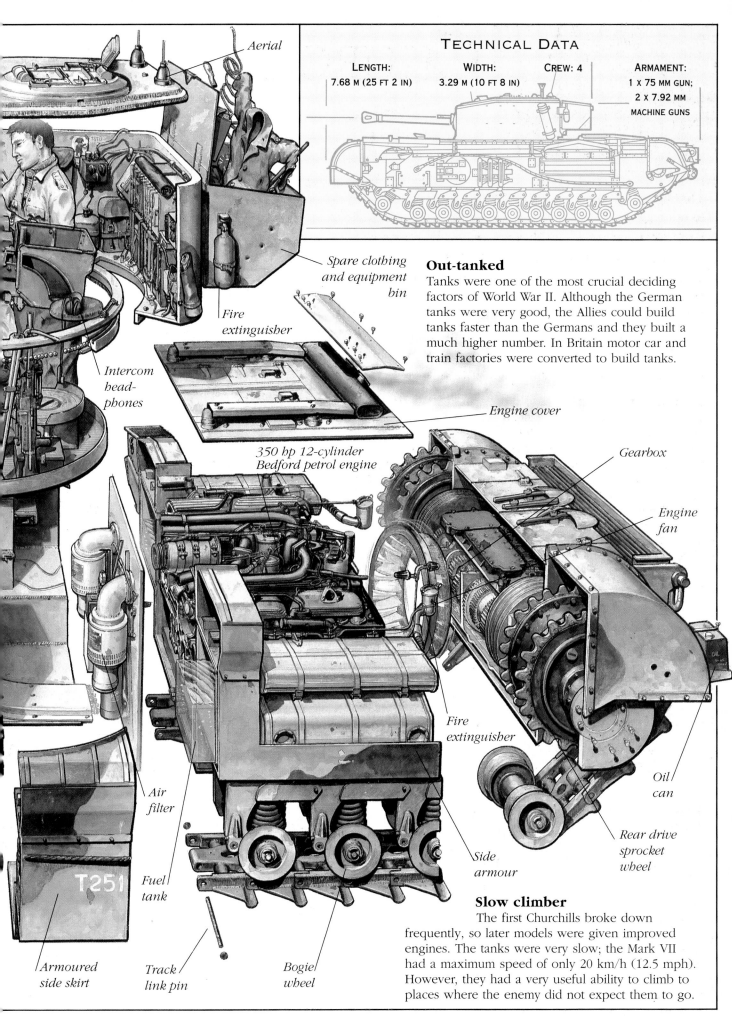

Aerial

TECHNICAL DATA

LENGTH:	WIDTH:	CREW: 4	ARMAMENT:
7.68 M (25 FT 2 IN)	3.29 M (10 FT 8 IN)		1 x 75 MM GUN; 2 x 7.92 MM MACHINE GUNS

Spare clothing and equipment bin

Fire extinguisher

Intercom head-phones

Out-tanked

Tanks were one of the most crucial deciding factors of World War II. Although the German tanks were very good, the Allies could build tanks faster than the Germans and they built a much higher number. In Britain motor car and train factories were converted to build tanks.

Engine cover

350 hp 12-cylinder Bedford petrol engine

Gearbox

Engine fan

Fire extinguisher

Oil can

Air filter

Side armour

Rear drive sprocket wheel

Armoured side skirt

Fuel tank

Track link pin

Bogie wheel

Slow climber

The first Churchills broke down frequently, so later models were given improved engines. The tanks were very slow; the Mark VII had a maximum speed of only 20 km/h (12.5 mph). However, they had a very useful ability to climb to places where the enemy did not expect them to go.

KING TIGER

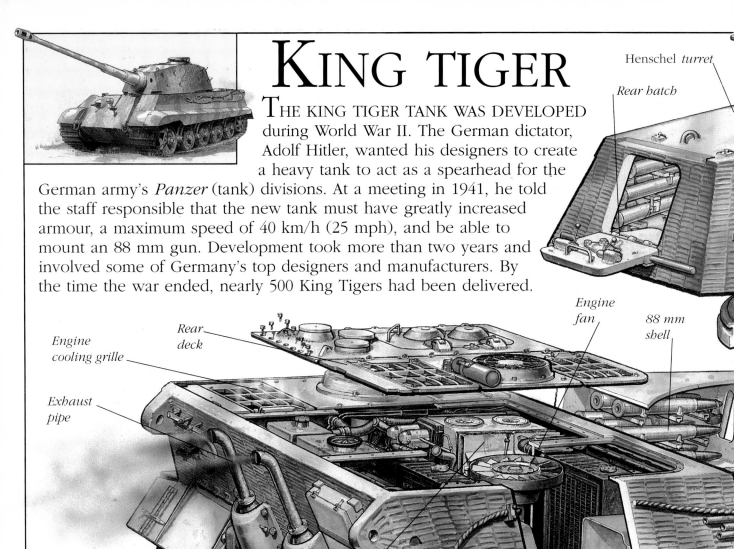

THE KING TIGER TANK WAS DEVELOPED during World War II. The German dictator, Adolf Hitler, wanted his designers to create a heavy tank to act as a spearhead for the German army's *Panzer* (tank) divisions. At a meeting in 1941, he told the staff responsible that the new tank must have greatly increased armour, a maximum speed of 40 km/h (25 mph), and be able to mount an 88 mm gun. Development took more than two years and involved some of Germany's top designers and manufacturers. By the time the war ended, nearly 500 King Tigers had been delivered.

Henschel *turret*

Rear *hatch*

Engine fan

88 mm shell

Rear deck

Engine cooling grille

Exhaust pipe

Exhaust silencer

Maybach HL230 P30 V12 700 hp petrol engine

Mudguard

Towing cable

"Zimmerit" anti-magnetic coating

Idler wheel

Fuel tank

Wheel hub

Road wheel arm

Firm footing
The King Tiger cruised on nine pairs of overlapped wheels. These were made of steel with rubber-covered rims. The 800 mm wide manganese steel tracks allowed the tank to cope with a wide variety of ground conditions.

Performance
The King Tiger was a tricky tank to maintain in battle conditions, needing frequent mechanical attention. This wasn't helped by the fact that the tank's drivers were often very inexperienced. Nevertheless, it was a formidable weapon. The combination of the 88 mm gun and thick armour made it very difficult for Allied forces to knock out.

Shell collection
Inside, the King Tiger had storage room for 64 rounds of 88 mm ammunition. Some of these were stowed in armoured bins in the sides of the tank and others inside the turret.

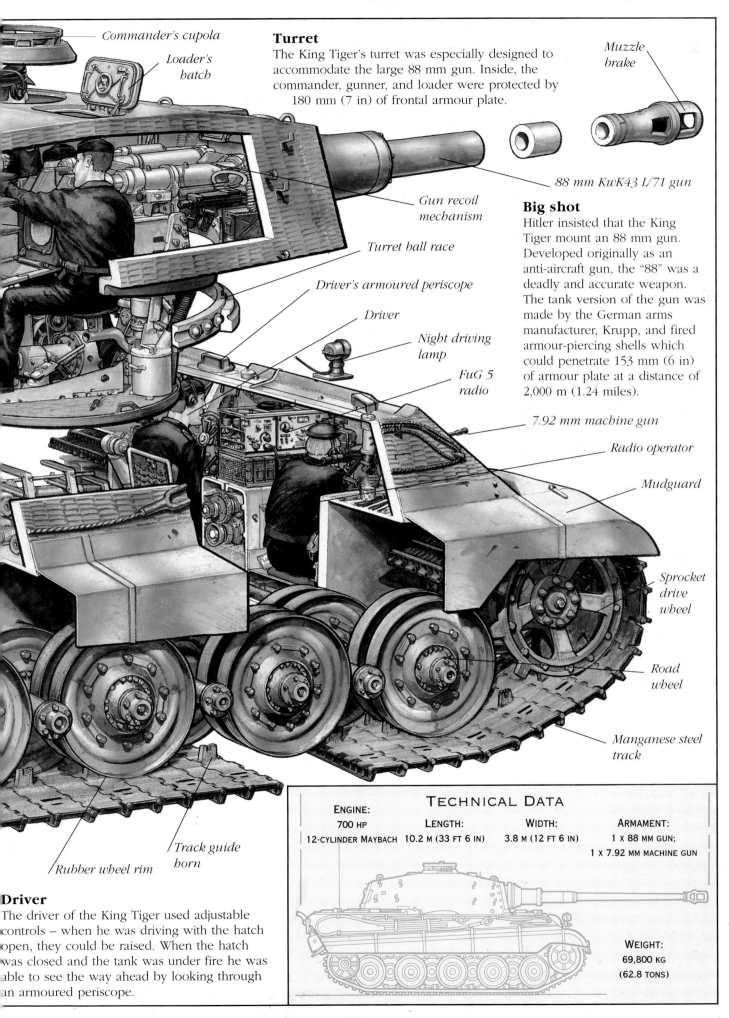

Commander's cupola

Loader's hatch

Turret
The King Tiger's turret was especially designed to accommodate the large 88 mm gun. Inside, the commander, gunner, and loader were protected by 180 mm (7 in) of frontal armour plate.

Muzzle brake

88 mm KwK43 I/71 gun

Gun recoil mechanism

Turret ball race

Driver's armoured periscope

Driver

Night driving lamp

FuG 5 radio

Big shot
Hitler insisted that the King Tiger mount an 88 mm gun. Developed originally as an anti-aircraft gun, the "88" was a deadly and accurate weapon. The tank version of the gun was made by the German arms manufacturer, Krupp, and fired armour-piercing shells which could penetrate 153 mm (6 in) of armour plate at a distance of 2,000 m (1.24 miles).

7.92 mm machine gun

Radio operator

Mudguard

Sprocket drive wheel

Road wheel

Manganese steel track

Track guide horn

Rubber wheel rim

Driver
The driver of the King Tiger used adjustable controls – when he was driving with the hatch open, they could be raised. When the hatch was closed and the tank was under fire he was able to see the way ahead by looking through an armoured periscope.

TECHNICAL DATA

ENGINE:	LENGTH:	WIDTH:	ARMAMENT:
700 HP 12-CYLINDER MAYBACH	10.2 M (33 FT 6 IN)	3.8 M (12 FT 6 IN)	1 x 88 MM GUN; 1 x 7.92 MM MACHINE GUN

WEIGHT: 69,800 KG (62.8 TONS)

SHERMAN

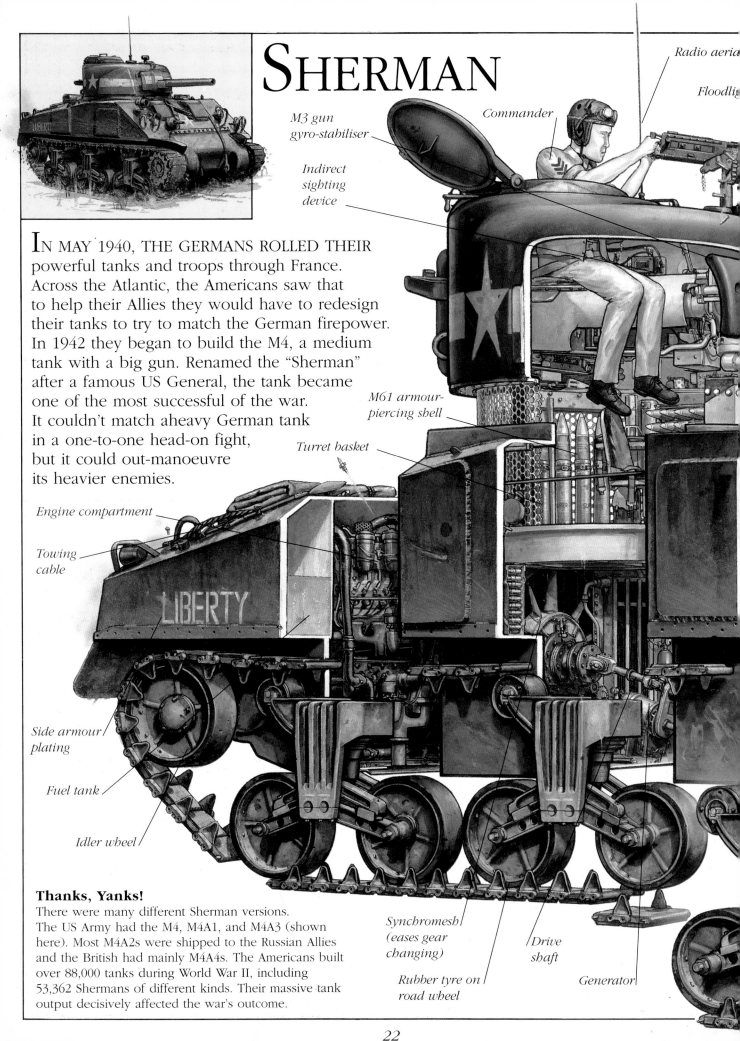

Radio aerial

Floodlig

Commander

M3 gun gyro-stabiliser

Indirect sighting device

IN MAY 1940, THE GERMANS ROLLED THEIR powerful tanks and troops through France. Across the Atlantic, the Americans saw that to help their Allies they would have to redesign their tanks to try to match the German firepower. In 1942 they began to build the M4, a medium tank with a big gun. Renamed the "Sherman" after a famous US General, the tank became one of the most successful of the war. It couldn't match aheavy German tank in a one-to-one head-on fight, but it could out-manoeuvre its heavier enemies.

M61 armour-piercing shell

Turret basket

Engine compartment

Towing cable

Side armour plating

Fuel tank

Idler wheel

Synchromesh (eases gear changing)

Drive shaft

Rubber tyre on road wheel

Generator

Thanks, Yanks!
There were many different Sherman versions. The US Army had the M4, M4A1, and M4A3 (shown here). Most M4A2s were shipped to the Russian Allies and the British had mainly M4A4s. The Americans built over 88,000 tanks during World War II, including 53,362 Shermans of different kinds. Their massive tank output decisively affected the war's outcome.

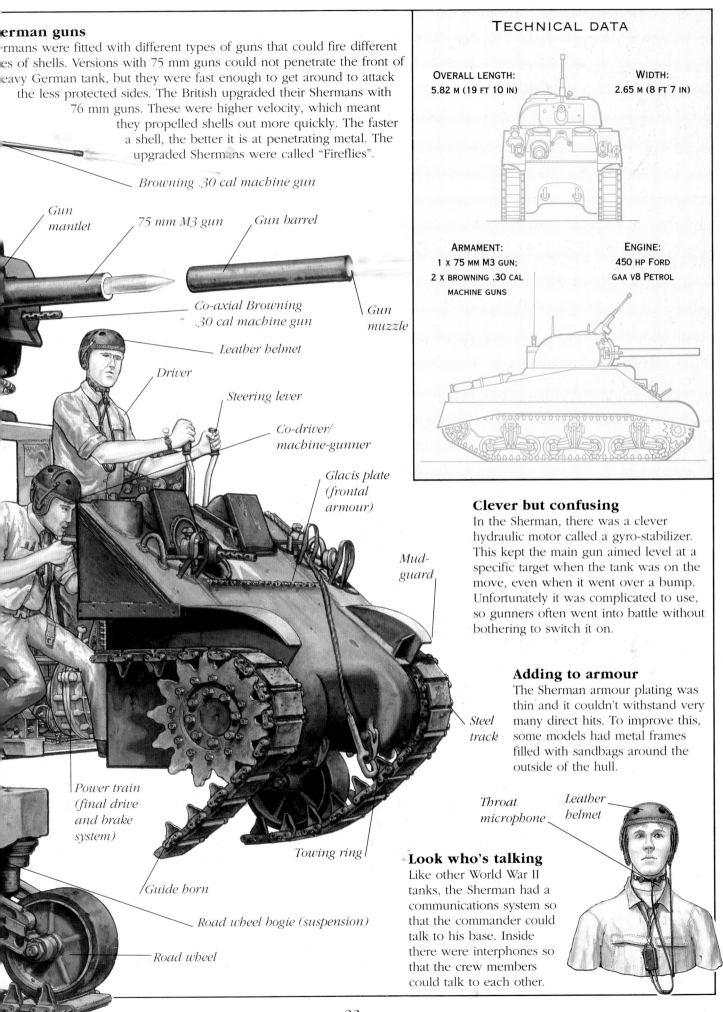

German guns

[Sher]mans were fitted with different types of guns that could fire different [typ]es of shells. Versions with 75 mm guns could not penetrate the front of [a h]eavy German tank, but they were fast enough to get around to attack the less protected sides. The British upgraded their Shermans with 76 mm guns. These were higher velocity, which meant they propelled shells out more quickly. The faster a shell, the better it is at penetrating metal. The upgraded Shermans were called "Fireflies".

Browning .30 cal machine gun

Gun mantlet

75 mm M3 gun

Gun barrel

Co-axial Browning .30 cal machine gun

Gun muzzle

Leather helmet

Driver

Steering lever

Co-driver/ machine-gunner

Glacis plate (frontal armour)

Mud-guard

Power train (final drive and brake system)

Steel track

Guide horn

Towing ring

Road wheel bogie (suspension)

Road wheel

TECHNICAL DATA

OVERALL LENGTH:
5.82 M (19 FT 10 IN)

WIDTH:
2.65 M (8 FT 7 IN)

ARMAMENT:
1 x 75 MM M3 GUN;
2 x BROWNING .30 CAL
MACHINE GUNS

ENGINE:
450 HP FORD
GAA V8 PETROL

Clever but confusing

In the Sherman, there was a clever hydraulic motor called a gyro-stabilizer. This kept the main gun aimed level at a specific target when the tank was on the move, even when it went over a bump. Unfortunately it was complicated to use, so gunners often went into battle without bothering to switch it on.

Adding to armour

The Sherman armour plating was thin and it couldn't withstand very many direct hits. To improve this, some models had metal frames filled with sandbags around the outside of the hull.

Throat microphone

Leather helmet

Look who's talking

Like other World War II tanks, the Sherman had a communications system so that the commander could talk to his base. Inside there were interphones so that the crew members could talk to each other.

M1 ABRAMS

TANKS HAVE DEVELOPED GREATLY SINCE the end of World War II. Now they have computer and laser technology, much better armour, and a new low, sleek outline. Their crews are much safer and more comfortable, a far cry from the stifling heat and overcrowding of the crews in those experimental days of early tanks. Designers spend years and huge budgets designing new tanks. An example is the American M1 Abrams, which took more than a decade to develop and was first delivered to the US Army in 1980. It was the most advanced tank design since World War II and it will probably be used into the 21st century. It saw combat during the Gulf War in 1991, destroying over 2,000 enemy tanks. Amazingly, not a single M1 was destroyed during the battle.

High-tech

Latest versions of the Abrams use technology adapted from aircraft to improve their performance. This includes the use of lasers to automatically calculate the distance (range) from the tank to a target. Other innovations being developed are laser devices to confuse enemy weapons systems, and identification beacons to prevent the tank being hit by "friendly fire" (shells from weapons of the same side).

Big bang

The heart of the Abrams's offensive capability is the 120 mm cannon. This fires "discarding sabot" rounds – once the shell is fired, the sides (sabots) drop away, leaving a rocket-shaped projectile which penetrates the enemy tank and then explodes.

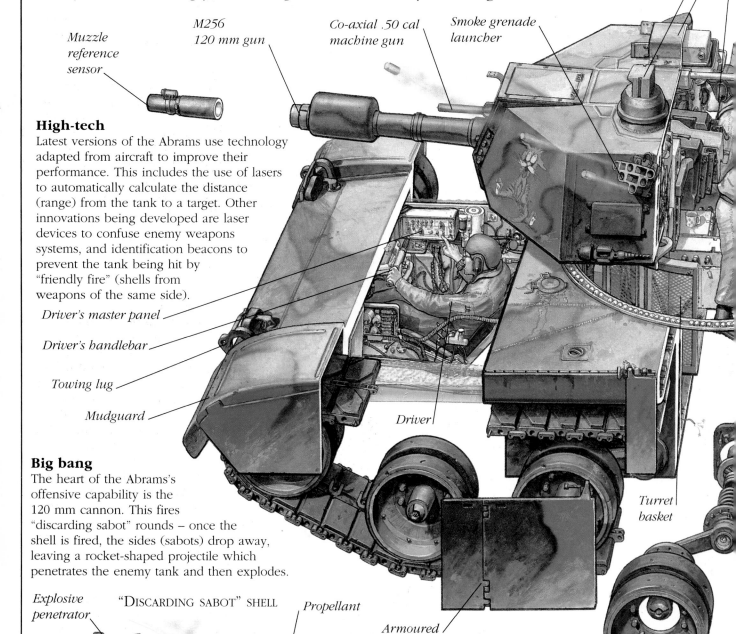

Commander's .50 cal machine gun

Gunner

Gunner's primary sight

Thermal viewer

Muzzle reference sensor

M256 120 mm gun

Co-axial .50 cal machine gun

Smoke grenade launcher

Driver's master panel

Driver's handlebar

Towing lug

Mudguard

Driver

Turret basket

Explosive penetrator

"DISCARDING SABOT" SHELL

Propellant

Armoured side skirt section

Road wheel with rubber tyre

Whe fixi bolt

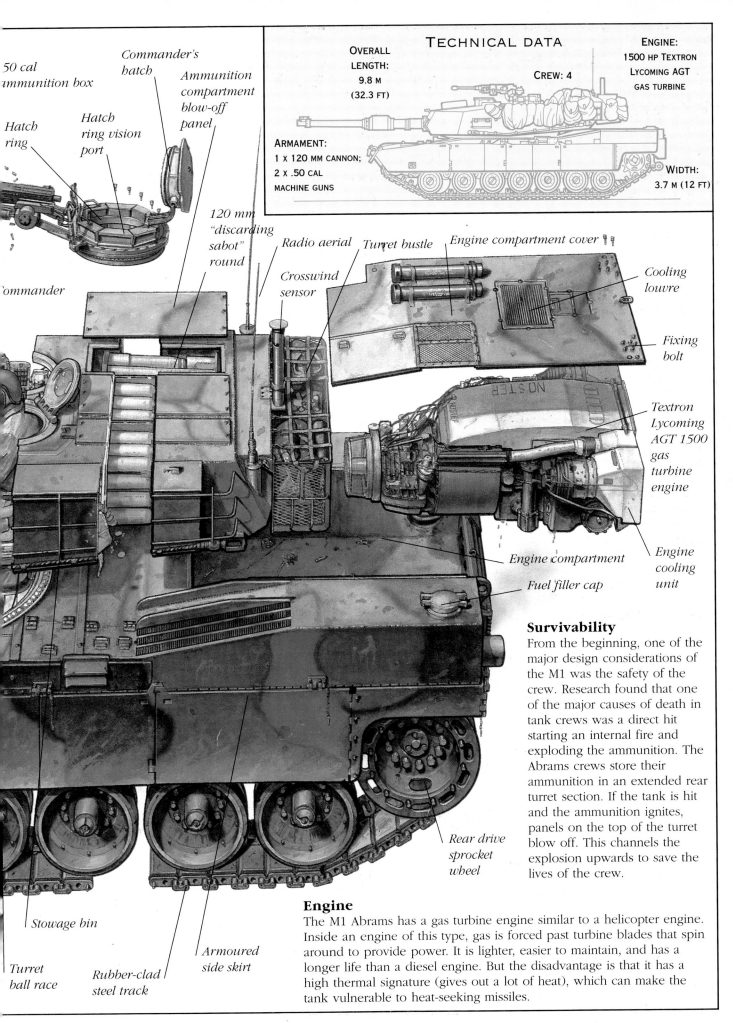

50 cal ammunition box

Commander's hatch

Ammunition compartment blow-off panel

Hatch ring

Hatch ring vision port

Commander

120 mm "discarding sabot" round

Radio aerial

Crosswind sensor

Turret bustle

Engine compartment cover

Cooling louvre

Fixing bolt

Textron Lycoming AGT 1500 gas turbine engine

Engine compartment

Engine cooling unit

Fuel filler cap

Rear drive sprocket wheel

Stowage bin

Turret ball race

Rubber-clad steel track

Armoured side skirt

TECHNICAL DATA

OVERALL LENGTH:
9.8 M
(32.3 FT)

CREW: 4

ENGINE:
1500 HP TEXTRON LYCOMING AGT GAS TURBINE

ARMAMENT:
1 x 120 MM CANNON;
2 x .50 CAL
MACHINE GUNS

WIDTH:
3.7 M (12 FT)

Survivability

From the beginning, one of the major design considerations of the M1 was the safety of the crew. Research found that one of the major causes of death in tank crews was a direct hit starting an internal fire and exploding the ammunition. The Abrams crews store their ammunition in an extended rear turret section. If the tank is hit and the ammunition ignites, panels on the top of the turret blow off. This channels the explosion upwards to save the lives of the crew.

Engine

The M1 Abrams has a gas turbine engine similar to a helicopter engine. Inside an engine of this type, gas is forced past turbine blades that spin around to provide power. It is lighter, easier to maintain, and has a longer life than a diesel engine. But the disadvantage is that it has a high thermal signature (gives out a lot of heat), which can make the tank vulnerable to heat-seeking missiles.

"FUNNIES"

During world war II, tanks were basically used as mobile armoured platforms to carry a big gun, either as an anti-tank weapon, or for helping the infantry. However, occasionally they were needed for other jobs and since there was no time to wait for new designs, existing tanks had to be adapted by engineers. The Sherman and the Churchill provided most of the variations, nicknamed "Funnies". Here are a few examples of their ingenuity.

The Churchill's bridge wasn't meant to be permanent, but it could be used until engineers built a more solid version.

CHURCHILL BRIDGELAYER

Wide water

World War II tanks worked best in flat open countryside and tactics became much more difficult when there were hedges or woods, streams or rivers. An ordinary tank could get stuck if it came to a river that was too wide and deep to cross. That's when a bridgelaying tank came in useful.

Huge arm swung bridge into place

Bridging the gap

The Churchill bridgelayer w a standard Churchill hull w the turret removed. In its place was a 9.14 m (30 ft) bridge which could be launched forward on a powerful hinged arm.

Counterweight

CHURCHILL "CROCODILE" FLAMETHROWER TANK

Difficult pills

German army engineers were good at building strong defensive positions. All along the Northern French coast, they built strong concrete pillboxes so they could fire on the Allies while staying under cover themselves.

Turret and hull looked like an ordinary Churchill

Fiery firepower

The British developed the Churchill as a flame-throwing tank which was successfully able to attack these obstacles. As well as its normal gun the tank had a flame gun mounted at the front. the back there was an armoured trailer with 1,818 litres (400 gallons) of flame fuel.

Armoured trailer contained flame fuel

The burning fuel was forced out of th flame gun by nitrogen gas under pressure

Flaming jet could travel 75 m (80 yards)

SHERMAN CRAB

Hidden danger

Tank tracks are very vulnerable parts. Damage to them could put a tank out of action however thick its armour or big its gun. One of the greatest threats to tracks in World War II were anti-tank mines that were buried just under the ground ready to detonate if a tank drove over them. These were laid in great numbers across areas called minefields.

Turret was reversed when clearing mines to protect gun

Steel arms supported cylinder

Flailing chains exploded mines in front of tank

Chains had steel balls on ends

Chains attached to spinning cylinder

Chain reaction

The Sherman Crab was fitted with a revolving cylinder fitted with chains and attached to the front of the hull. The cylinder was driven around by the tank's engine power and the chains flailed the ground in front, setting off mines and gradually clearing a path through a minefield.

SHERMAN DD (DUPLEX DRIVE)

Attack by sea

During the war, Allied armies landed troops and equipment from the sea on to enemy-held territory. To get ashore they needed amphibious tanks that could move in water and on land. The Sherman DD was equipped with two propellers at the back, connected to the main gearbox. This gave the tank a speed of about knots through the water.

Collapsible screen made the Sherman waterproof

Propellers pushed tank through water

Drop the screen

A collapsible screen was attached around the tank's hull. It stretched up above the turret and all around the tank, helping it to float after it was launched from a ship. When the tank reached land a small explosive charge ripped the screen away and the tank went into battle. Tanks of this type were landed at the beginning of an amphibious assault to hold the landing places until heavier tank landing craft could get to shore.

Screen in collapsed position

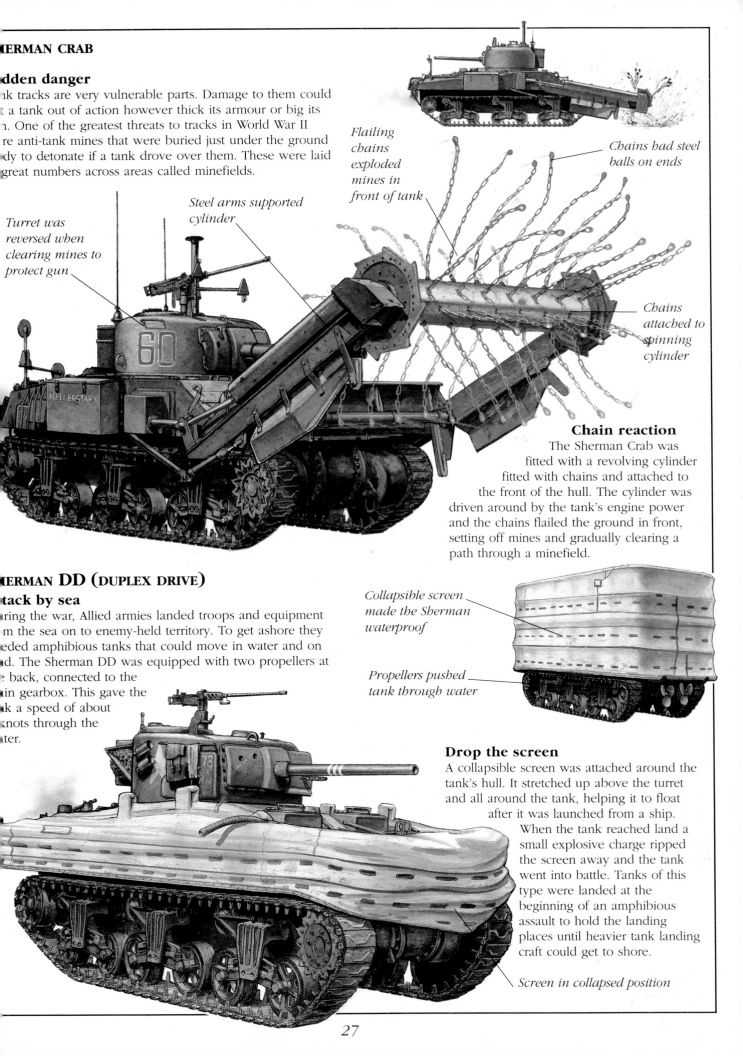

GLOSSARY

Ammunition
Shells and bullets stored in a tank and loaded into its guns during battle.

Amphibious tank
A tank that can travel through water as well as on land. This is useful when armies must make an amphibious landing, landing troops from ships on to land.

Anti-tank mine
Explosive charge buried beneath the ground and set off by the pressure of a tank driving over it.

Armament
All the different types of guns a tank has on board.

Armour
Thick steel plating that helps to protect a tank from bullets and shells. Its thickness varies on different tank types.

Barbette
A small turret raised above the body, used in early tanks before revolving turrets were made.

Basket
A structure inside the hull, hanging down below the turret and revolving around with it. The turret crew and their equipment sit in the basket.

Blitzkrieg
The German World War II tactic of sending tank divisions racing into enemy territory to split up the enemy forces. Infantry then marched in behind the tanks.

Bogies
Wheel mountings that link the wheels of a tank. They help support the weight of the tank's body.

Bridgelayer
A tank carrying a folded-up bridge. It can extend the bridge and lower it down over an obstacle such as a river. Later, the tank can come back and pick its bridge up to use again.

Bustle
The overhanging back part of a tank turret, usually used to store ammunition or radio equipment.

Calibre
The diameter of a shell that can be fired by a gun. For instance, an 88 mm gun can fire a shell that is 88 mm across.

Chassis
The frame on to which a tank body is fixed.

Cupola
An extra section raised above a tank turret, from which the commander can look out.

Drive sprocket
A toothed wheel that is turned by the power of the engine. As it moves it drives a tank crawler track around.

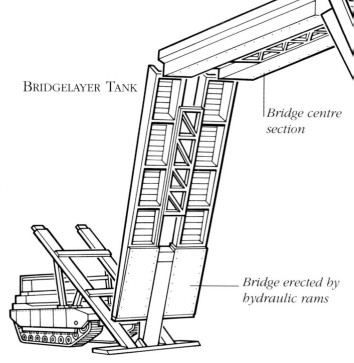

BRIDGELAYER TANK

Bridge centre section

Bridge erected by hydraulic rams

Fascine
A large roll of brushwood wrapped in wire. Some tanks can carry these and drop them into ditches. The fascines fill up the ditches so that tanks can drive across them.

Gas turbine engine
An engine in which gas is forced past turbine blades, making them spin around to generate power.

Grousers
Metal plates bolted on top of tank tracks to give them extra grip on slippery surfaces such as snow and mud.

Gun emplacement
A building or structure built of sandbags where a guncrew can shelter, aiming their gun at the enemy. Tanks are used to destroy gun emplacements.

Gyro-stabilizer
A hydraulically powered motor used to keep a b gun pointed level at a target, even when a tan is on the move.

Hatch
A small door used for getting in and out of a tank or for seeing outsid

Hull
The main body of a tank above the tracks. Different types of tanks have differently shaped hulls.

Idler
A wheel inside one end of a tank track. It turns freely as the track moves round.

Infantry
Army foot soldiers. During both World Wars, tanks and infantry worked together on the battlefield.

Infantry tank
A slow and heavily armoured tank used to protect infantry.

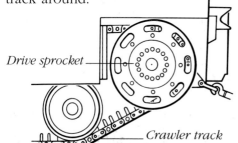

Drive sprocket

Crawler track

Roadway for vehicles

Machine gun
A gun that shoots a continuous stream of bullets in one firing.

Muzzle
Barrel
Breech

.50 CALIBRE MACHINE GUN

Night vision device
Used to detect infra-red light emissions at night, or to electronically improve ordinary light so a tank crew can see better.

Panzers
The German word for armour. It came to mean German tanks and also German tank divisions during World War II.

Periscope
Optical equipment that a crew member uses to see outside a tank, while sitting inside in safety.

Petrol engine
An engine in which a petrol and air mixture is burnt, making gases that push pistons up and down, generating power. Diesel engines need diesel fuel instead of petrol to make them work.

Pistol ports
Small plugged openings along a tank, which can be unplugged so that the crew can fire revolvers out of them to defend themselves.

Range
A word used in three different ways: how far a gun can fire; the distance between a gun and its target; and the distance a tank can travel before it runs out of fuel.

Return rollers
Small wheels that support the upper part of a tank track.

Tracks
Continuous loops of metal links running around rollers on either side of a tank.

Transmission
The parts of a tank that transfer power from the engine to the tracks.

Traverse
The distance a gun can swing from side to side when it is mounted on a tank turret. Also the distance a turret can rotate.

Trenches
Long ditches dug across the battlefields of World War I. Troops sheltered in them, protected by barbed wire and mounds of sloping earth called parapets.

Turret
The top part of a tank that holds a big gun. It usually rotates.

...ra-red
...t of a ray of light, a ...t that can't be seen ...the human eye. ...jects give off infra-...l rays; the warmer ...y are the more they ...e off. Electronic tank ...uipment can detect ...ra-red light and find ...iding enemy.

...terphones
...uipment the crew ...e to talk to each ...er inside the tank.

...ser
...narrow concentrated ...am of light that can ...very accurately ...ected at a target to ...npoint it and ...asure its distance ...m a tank.

...ght tank
...lightweight fast ...nk armed only with ...achine guns.

...uvres
...ts above a tank's ...gine compartment ...ich let engine ...at escape.

Medium tank
A tank armed with a medium sized gun and machine guns.

Muzzle brake
A part fitted to the muzzle (front) of a gun. When a shell is fired, gases trail out behind it. The brake deflects the gases away from the gun, to reduce the gun's recoil (backwards jolt).

Muzzle velocity
The speed of a shell or a bullet as it leaves the muzzle of a gun. It is measured in metres or feet per second.

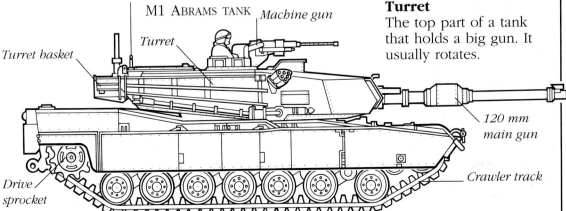

M1 ABRAMS TANK
Machine gun
Turret
Turret basket
120 mm main gun
Crawler track
Drive sprocket

INDEX

Acknowledgments

Dorling Kindersley would like
thank the following people wh
helped with the preparation of
this book:

Gary Biggin for line artworks
Lynn Bresler for the index
Constance Novis for editorial supp
Paul Wood for DTP design